# GUIDED WRITER'S NOTEBOOK

An Instructional Journal to Plan Your Story

BY LIZ DELTON

# GUIDED WRITER'S NOTEBOOK

an instructional journal to plan your story

Written and Created by

Liz Delton

First Edition

ISBN 978-1-7345231-4-0



Tourmaline & Quartz Publishing

P. O. Box 193, North Granby, CT 06060

* * *

Comments and suggestions for the next edition are welcome at liz@lizdelton.com

Visit MyWritersNotebook.com for more writing resources

# HOW TO USE THIS NOTEBOOK

## Start anywhere

The next page lists all the different sections of the notebook. Start anywhere, but come back to the Idea section if you get stuck.

## Skip around

Don't feel like you have to fill out everything, especially not all at once. If you get stuck on one thing, skip to another section. You can always go back.

## Write, draw, doodle, anything

There are lots of blank pages for you to make notes in. Sketch your characters, settings, objects from your story if you like—it doesn't have to be perfect.

## Need help?

...For writer's block, check out page 10

...For writing tips, go to page 95

...For more writer resources, visit MyWritersNotebook.com

## Now, write your story!

# TABLE OF CONTENTS

**IDEAS**......5
Idea Generator/Writer's Block......10
**PROJECT**......15
Title......16
About the Project......17
**STORY**......19
Conflict Makes A Story......20
One Line Story Concept......22
Story Premise......23
Three Act Structure......24
Hero's Journey......26
Subplots......30
Action Beats......31
Story Calendar......34
Story Grids......36
**CHARACTERS**......49
Writing Great Characters......50
Character Profiles......52
Character List......64
Family Trees......66
Character Name Ideas......68
**SETTING**......73
Setting Profile......74
Maps & Drawings......78
Place Name Ideas......82
**GOALS**......87
Word Count Goals......88
Goals and Progress......90
**WRITING TIPS**......95
How to Write......96
Writing & Editing Process......97
Wordsmithing......98
Writing Conversations......100
Writing the Senses......102
Show Don't Tell......103
Writing FAQ......104
**NOTES** & Drawing Space......107

# IDEAS

# IDEAS

Use these pages to write down any ideas you have for your story. Don't worry about putting them in order yet, just write them down as you think of them. Later in the notebook you can focus on organizing, but for now, just write or even draw any ideas here.

# IDEAS

# Stuck?

It happens to everybody. Use the tools on the next few pages to help come up with ideas.

**Block Writer's Block** Want to write, but the words just won't come out? Try doing these things to get unstuck:

- Go for a walk
- Draw, paint, sculpt, or do something else creative
- Make a writing playlist
- Disconnect from all your devices
- Try writing on paper instead
- Read a book
- Fill in details in this notebook
- Draw (or write a description of) a setting in your story
- Make a cup of tea or coffee, or your favorite beverage
- Talk to a friend about your story
- Write a different short story or poem
- Check out page 20 for what makes a good story

**Word prompt** Need a story idea? Close your eyes and pick three words on this page. Then, write a sentence using all three words. Now try to write a story based off that sentence. Or, use the three words to come up with a title.

| Secret | Gold | Web | First |
|---|---|---|---|
| Glimpse | Flower | Song | Hidden |
| Calm | Shadow | Below | Small |
| Thousand | Sky | Wonder | Pretend |
| Footprints | Run | Cold | Proud |
| Sidewalk | Stone | Danger | Knock |
| Remember | Key | Smile | Unusual |
| Leaf | Wall | Flash | Everything |
| Find | Turn | Walk | Beautiful |
| Blue | Silver | Clock | Sunset |
| Time | Tree | Window | Road |
| Charming | Mesmerizing | Bark | Answer |
| Betray | Hint | Lost | Never |
| Agony | Closed | Open | Familiar |
| Green | Whisper | Never | Bargain |
| Together | Grey | Fast | Asleep |
| Dark | Sharp | Stolen | Discover |
| Clear | Night | Broken | Fragile |
| Home | Desperate | Stop | Simple |
| Silent | Wish | Strange | Always |
| Escape | Howl | Protect | Courage |
| Absurd | Nothing | Trouble | Artist |
| Sleepy | Purpose | Quick | Demand |
| Ferocious | Freezing | Deny | Promise |
| Sinister | Jewel | Shriek | Sparkle |
| Strong | Letter | Exhausted | Complicated |
| Ocean | Wonder | Generous | Thunder |

# IDEA GENERATOR

**Idea Map** Have a story idea but don't know what to do? Fill in the bubbles with your thoughts to form the big picture. Start in the center with the main idea of what the story is about.

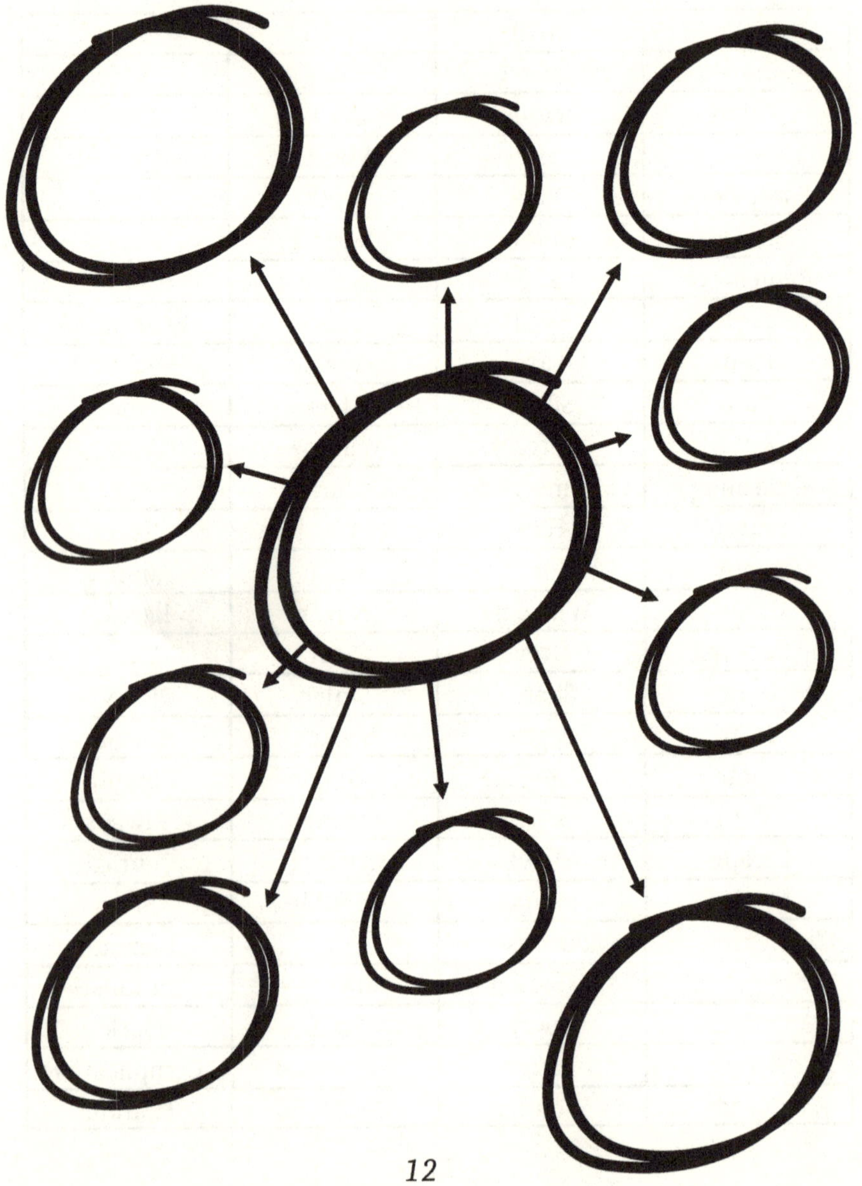

You can also draw your own idea map here.

# MORE IDEAS

# PROJECT

# PROJECT TITLE

If you don't have a title for your story already, don't worry. You don't need the title to get started on writing. Use this page to write down ideas for the story title as they come to you, then circle your favorites.

Title:

# ABOUT THE PROJECT

**Point of View** (also known as POV) Whose perspective is the story written from?

❍ **First Person**

Example: *I lifted my hand to grab the notebook off the shelf. "This is mine," I said, showing it to Alex.*

Uses: I, Me, My

Rules: What one character sees and thinks.

❍ **Third Person**

Example: *Liam took the notebook off the shelf. "This is mine," he said, wanting Alex to see what he wrote.*

Uses: She/He, Her/His, They

Rules: What one character experiences, but not told using "I".

❍ **Multiple**

Example: *"Liam took the notebook and said, "This is mine." He wanted Alex to see what he wrote.*

*But Alex wasn't interested in Liam's notebook, he was more interested in the strange shadow by the door.*

Uses: She/He, Her/His, They

Rules: Can hop from character to character, usually between chapters so it doesn't get confusing.

## Genre

**Genre** is the general category your story fits into. What section in the library or bookstore would it be placed in?

- ❍ Contemporary
- ❍ Romance
- ❍ Fantasy
- ❍ SCIENCE FICTION
- ❍ Historical
- ❍ Thriller
- ❍ HORROR
- ❍ MYSTERY
- ❍ Something else:______________________________

## Subgenre

**Subgenre** is the more specific type of story. For example, a book might belong in the *Science Fiction* genre, but the subgenre could be *dystopian*, *space travel*, or even *aliens*.

________________________________________

## Audience

Who do you want to read your story? Is it for adults, teens, children, or any specific age or demographic? Knowing this from the beginning will help you write with your audience in mind.

________________________________________

# STORY

# CONFLICT MAKES A STORY

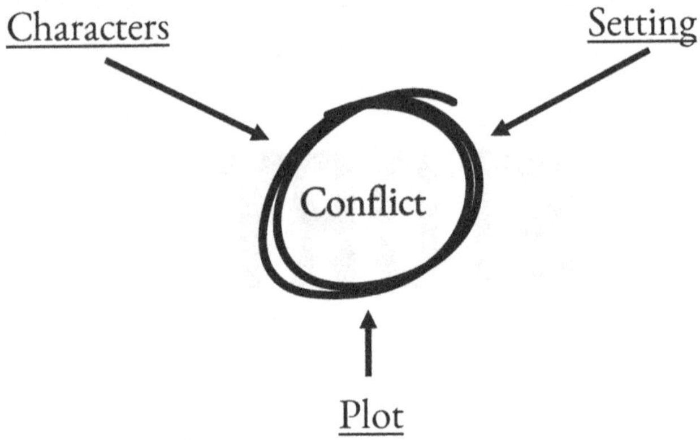


**Characters** are directly involved in a conflict. Your main character will be invested in the outcome of the conflict—their life, or their dreams, or their wants and needs are on the line. Characters will change somehow throughout the story because of the conflict.

**Setting** can also inform the conflict. Perhaps your character is being oppressed by the society they live or work in. The setting can also be changed through conflict (the characters might overthrow an oppressive government, for example).

**Plot** is the storyline that moves all of these elements forward. It is how your character gets from point A to point Z. Plot can create unexpected problems for both characters and settings.

**Conflict** is created by all of these elements coming together. It is the reason the story is being told.

There are several widely known types of conflict. Which kind will your story be?

## Character vs. Character

The conflict is between two characters or more.

## Character vs. Nature

The conflict could be with an animal, the climate, survival in harsh weather, etc.

## Character vs. Society

Be it the government, conflicting with what's perceived as normal in society, or fighting against a flaw in society.

## Character vs. Technology

From science (an invention gone wrong) to problems with machinery (stranded on a space ship), and more.

## Character vs. Supernatural

Anything that is unexplained: ghosts, fate, gods, etc.

## Character vs. Self

Generally an internal struggle against one's own weaknesses, personality, or motivations.

# ONE LINE STORY CONCEPT

**Story concept** is putting your story idea into the vaguest terms possible. Try writing a few one line story concepts for your story.

Some examples of story concepts:

- Two people fall in love.
- A man moves to a new town.
- A girl befriends a dragon.

## STORY PREMISE

A **premise** is a more specific version of your concept. The premise is like looking at an object close up, instead of from far away. Try writing your premise using up to three sentences, expanding on the one line concept from before. An example of a premise:

*Kyla Marks finds an injured dragon in the woods behind her school one day. She takes care of it only to realize it's being hunted by something. She must figure out a way to protect her dragon or risk her own life.*

# THREE ACT STRUCTURE

The three act structure is a classic way of storytelling, just like in theatre. When writing, each act won't necessarily be the same length—and Act Two is usually where most of the action is. Draw your own structure on the next page and label key events.

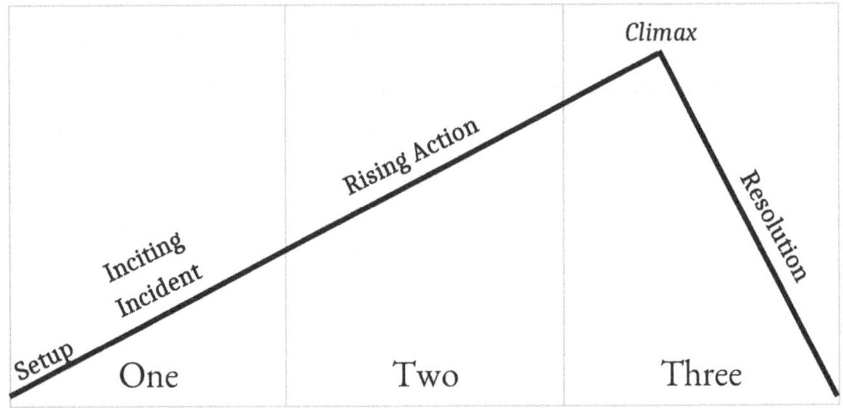


Act 1

Setup: Also known as exposition, where the main character and the world are established.

Inciting Incident: This is the catalyst that sets the main character on their journey into the story.

Act 2

Rising Action: The character encounters problems (that only get worse) as a result of the inciting incident. They also discover/work on new skills to deal with those problems.

Act 3

Climax: The most intense point in the story conflict.

Resolution: All plots and subplots are resolved, generally leaving the character to reflect on how they have changed as a person as a result of the conflict and its resolution.

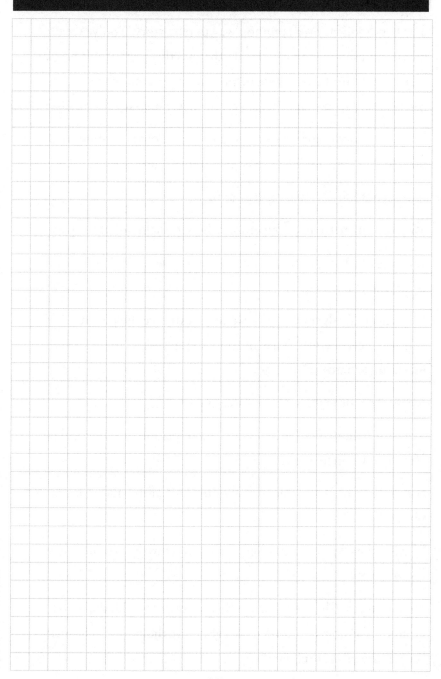

# HERO'S JOURNEY

The hero's journey is a common way to tell a story. You've seen movies and shows, and read books that use this pattern. It's not for every story, but the basics are helpful to understand when constructing your main characters' journey, especially for fantasy.

**The Call to Adventure**: The hero starts the story going about their ordinary life, but are called to go on an adventure.

**Refusal of Call**: The hero refuses at first.

**Mentor**: The hero meets a mentor, who sets them down the path.

**Crossing the Threshold**: The hero leaves the world he knows and enters the Unknown.

**Challenges**: Trials challenge the hero, but they get help from **allies**, and also meet **enemies**. They must master **new skills** to overcome increasingly harder challenges.

**Abyss**: The ultimate confrontation or trial.

**Transformation**: The hero undergoes a revelation or transformation after their ultimate trial.

**Gift or Reward**: The achievement of the goal of the quest, or even a physical gift.

**The Road Back**: The hero might refuse to return at first, but they return anyway.

**Hero Returns, Changed**: Back in their ordinary world, the hero has grown and changed, but they now also have the ability to return to the Unknown world if it arises.

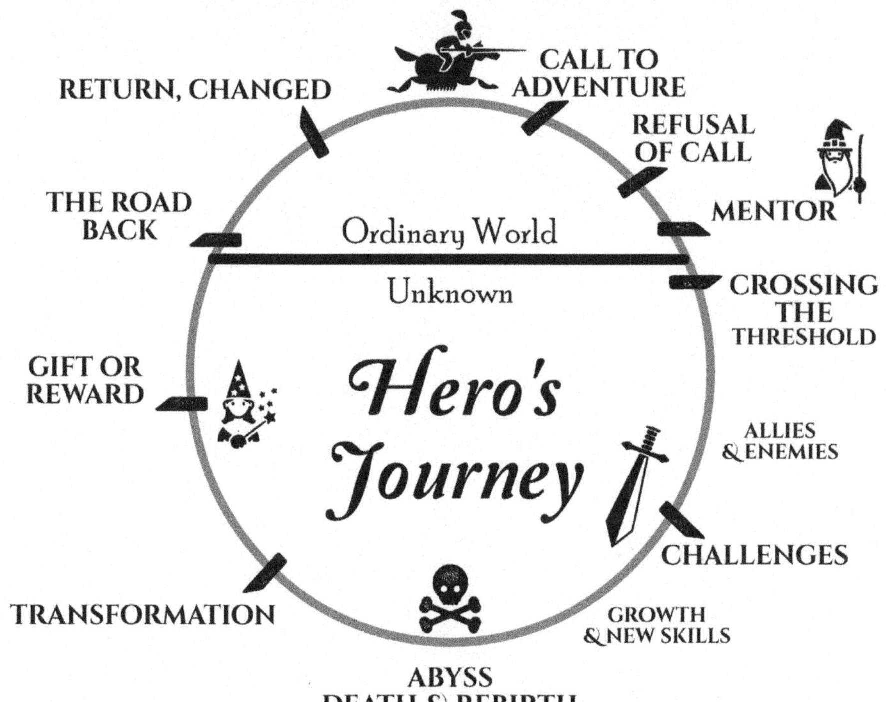

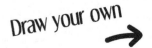

Draw your own →

## DRAWING SPACE

# SUBPLOTS

Almost every story contains subplots, or storylines that are separate from the main plot, but are intertwined. A good subplot should be **relevant to the events of the main storyline**, and help **show development of your characters.**

Some examples of types of subplots:

- Romantic interests
- An achievement or a goal your main character is attempting
- A conflict between your main character and another
- Something going wrong in the setting

## Write any ideas for your own subplots here:

# ACTION BEATS

You can outline your entire story just by listing all of the **actions** that are going to happen. Actions *move* the plot forward. They should have an action verb, like in the examples below.

Later, when you're writing your story, one bullet point might take up three chapters, or, one chapter might contain the actions of five bullet points. Plotting this way will help you focus on moving your story forward though, so don't worry about chapters until later. Check out these few examples to start:

- Kyla **leaves** for school along the forest path
- Kyla **discovers** a baby dragon
- Kyla **brings** the dragon to a cave
- Kyla **confronts** Erin

# ACTION BEATS

- 
- 
- 
- 
- 
- 
- 
- 
- 
- 
- 

# STORY CALENDAR

Use these pages as a calendar for your story. Does it take place over several days, weeks, months, or years?

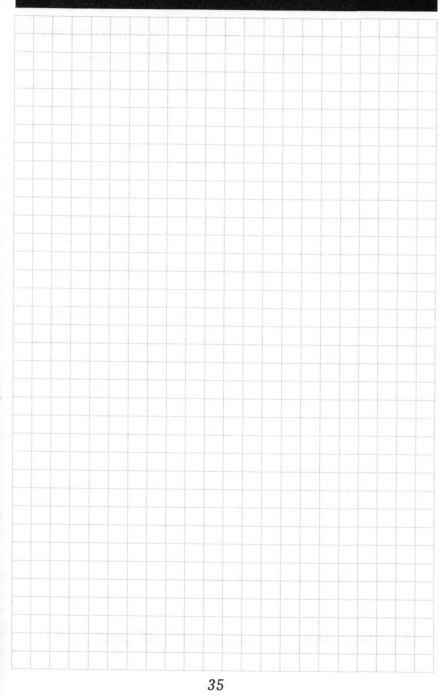

# STORY GRIDS

The next pages contain grids for plotting, or, for helping organize or revise after you've written your story. Not all grids may work for you or your story, and you don't have to use them all. On this page, you can see how the grids work:

## Plotline Grid

Plan and track how each plotline develops in each chapter. Fill in the top row with your characters' names and any subplots. Throughout each chapter, describe how they develop to see the whole arc. (Cross off the titles if they don't work for you, and write in your own.)

| | Main Conflict | MC's Journey | Villain's Journey | Subplot |
|---|---|---|---|---|
| 1 | Kyla discovers the injured baby dragon | Kyla doesn't know what to do about it | The hunters left the dragon in the woods | Kyla's friend Erin has been acting strange |
| 2 | Kyla has to find a way to carry the dragon | She is going to get in trouble for skipping school | | |
| 3 | Kyla takes the dragon to a place in the woods | | The hunters ransack Kyla's house | |
| 4 | | Kyla confronts Erin | | Erin is keeping a secret |

*MC stands for "Main Character"

(If you need more room to fill out your grids, go to page 44)

## Character Grid

This one is pretty easy, and is better for during or after you've written your story. Plan and track where the characters appear in each chapter.

| | 1 | 2 | 3 | 4 | 5 | 6 |
|---|---|---|---|---|---|---|
| **Kyla** | X | X | X | X | X | X |
| **Baby dragon** | X | X | | | X | |
| **Erin** | X | | | X | | |

## Scene Grid

Plan and track where each chapter takes place, and the key action that occurs in that chapter.

| | Setting | Action |
|---|---|---|
| 1 | The forest path | Kyla stumbles across the dragon on her way to school. |
| 2 | The forest path/back at Kyla's house | Deciding to rescue the dragon, Kyla goes to find something to carry it. |
| 3 | The cave in the forest/ Kyla's house | Kyla hides the dragon in the woods, and when she goes home her house has been searched. |

## STORY GRIDS—Plotline Grid

| | Main Conflict | Main Character's Journey |
|---|---|---|
| 1 | | |
| 2 | | |
| 3 | | |
| 4 | | |
| 5 | | |
| 6 | | |
| 7 | | |
| 8 | | |
| 9 | | |
| 10 | | |
| 11 | | |
| 12 | | |

| Villain's Journey | Subplot |
| --- | --- |
| | |
| | |
| | |
| | |
| | |
| | |
| | |
| | |
| | |
| | |
| | |
| | |

# STORY GRIDS—Character Grid

| Character | 1 | 2 | 3 | 4 | 5 | 6 | 7 | 8 | 9 | 10 | 11 | 12 |
|---|---|---|---|---|---|---|---|---|---|---|---|---|
| | | | | | | | | | | | | |
| | | | | | | | | | | | | |
| | | | | | | | | | | | | |
| | | | | | | | | | | | | |
| | | | | | | | | | | | | |
| | | | | | | | | | | | | |
| | | | | | | | | | | | | |
| | | | | | | | | | | | | |
| | | | | | | | | | | | | |
| | | | | | | | | | | | | |
| | | | | | | | | | | | | |
| | | | | | | | | | | | | |
| | | | | | | | | | | | | |
| | | | | | | | | | | | | |
| | | | | | | | | | | | | |
| | | | | | | | | | | | | |
| | | | | | | | | | | | | |
| | | | | | | | | | | | | |
| | | | | | | | | | | | | |

| 13 | 14 | 15 | 16 | 17 | 18 | 19 | 20 | 21 | 22 | 23 | 24 | 25 | 26 | 27 | 28 | 29 | 30 |
|---|---|---|---|---|---|---|---|---|---|---|---|---|---|---|---|---|---|
| | | | | | | | | | | | | | | | | | |
| | | | | | | | | | | | | | | | | | |
| | | | | | | | | | | | | | | | | | |
| | | | | | | | | | | | | | | | | | |
| | | | | | | | | | | | | | | | | | |
| | | | | | | | | | | | | | | | | | |
| | | | | | | | | | | | | | | | | | |
| | | | | | | | | | | | | | | | | | |
| | | | | | | | | | | | | | | | | | |
| | | | | | | | | | | | | | | | | | |
| | | | | | | | | | | | | | | | | | |
| | | | | | | | | | | | | | | | | | |
| | | | | | | | | | | | | | | | | | |
| | | | | | | | | | | | | | | | | | |
| | | | | | | | | | | | | | | | | | |
| | | | | | | | | | | | | | | | | | |
| | | | | | | | | | | | | | | | | | |
| | | | | | | | | | | | | | | | | | |
| | | | | | | | | | | | | | | | | | |

# STORY GRIDS—Scene Grid

| | Setting |
|---|---|
| 1 | |
| 2 | |
| 3 | |
| 4 | |
| 5 | |
| 6 | |
| 7 | |
| 8 | |
| 9 | |
| 10 | |
| 11 | |
| 12 | |
| 13 | |
| 14 | |
| 15 | |

| Main Action |
| --- |
| |
| |
| |
| |
| |
| |
| |
| |
| |
| |
| |
| |
| |
| |
| |

# FREE OUTLINE

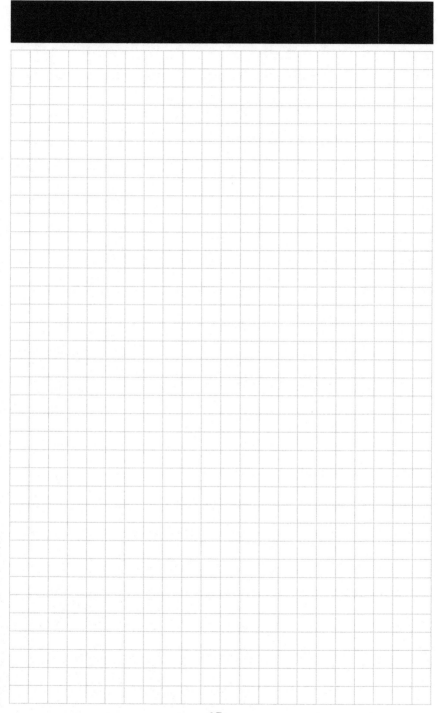

## MORE STORY NOTES

## MORE STORY NOTES

# CHARACTERS

## Some Character Terms

Main Character= MC

Protagonist: Leading or main character

Antagonist: A villain; they antagonize the protagonist.

Supporting Characters: Characters who help the protagonist along their journey.

Character Arc: The emotional/personal journey that a character takes throughout the story, causing them to grow as a person.

## Flaws and Strengths

To make a character believable, they can't be the best at everything; they need to have flaws. The flaws might be emotional, social, or part of their personality. For example, you might have a brave and strong character, but maybe she panics when things get complicated, and makes mistakes because of it.

## Your Characters' Goals

The main character's goal should be directly related to the conflict of the story, and what propels the story—Even if their goal is just to live a normal life or to stay alive, but to do so they have to enter conflict after conflict because outside forces are stopping them from their goal.

# Character-Driven Plot

The following chart will help you figure out your main characters' motivations, which should also help you develop your plot.

| Protagonist name: | |
|---|---|
| What is their goal? What would make them happy in life? | |
| What is stopping them from achieving their goal? | |

**Tip-** If you ever get stuck figuring out where the story should go, ask yourself: What is the worst thing that could happen to this character right now?

# CHARACTER PROFILES

There are three 4-page character profiles in this book. Fill in as much as you want about your important characters.

## The Basics: Who They Are

| Character Name: |
|---|
| Meaning behind the name (if any): |
| Nicknames or Titles: |
| Age and Gender Identity: |

## The Details

| Clothing and any special accessories: |
|---|
| What do they look like? |
| Job and/or school status: |
| Hobbies or skills: |
| Three words to describe them: |
| What is their personality like? |
| Where do they live? |

## Connections

| Family: |
|---|
| Friends and/or allies: |
| Romantic interest/relationship: |

## Deep Down: Who They Are

| What is special about them? |
|---|
| Do they have any secrets? |
| What are they afraid of? |
| How do they react when things go wrong? |

More on this character

## ...continued

| Character Name: |
|---|

## How They Fit Into The Story

| What motivates them? (who or what makes them take action?) |
|---|
| What are their limitations? (what is holding them back from getting what they want?) |
| What are their strengths as a person? What are they good at? |
| What are their weaknesses or flaws? What are they bad at? |
| How will they change/grow as a person during the story? |

# Draw Your Character

Or use this space for photos/celebrity casting

# CHARACTER PROFILES

## The Basics: Who They Are

| Character Name: |
|---|
| Meaning behind the name (if any): |
| Nicknames or Titles: |
| Age and Gender Identity: |

## The Details

| Clothing and any special accessories: |
|---|
| What do they look like? |
| Job and/or school status: |
| Hobbies or skills: |
| Three words to describe them: |
| What is their personality like? |
| Where do they live? |

## Connections

| Family: |
|---|
| Friends and/or allies: |
| Romantic interest/relationship: |

## Deep Down: Who They Are

| What is special about them? |
|---|
| Do they have any secrets? |
| What are they afraid of? |
| How do they react when things go wrong? |

More on this character →

## ...continued

| Character Name: |
|---|

## How They Fit Into The Story

| What motivates them? (who or what makes them take action?) |
|---|
| What are their limitations? (what is holding them back from getting what they want?) |
| What are their strengths as a person? What are they good at? |
| What are their weaknesses or flaws? What are they bad at? |
| How will they change/grow as a person during the story? |

## Draw Your Character

Or use this space for photos/celebrity casting

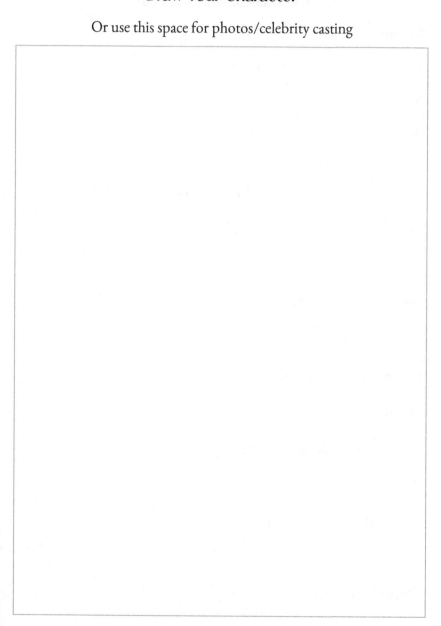

# CHARACTER PROFILES

## The Basics: Who They Are

| Character Name: |
| --- |
| Meaning behind the name (if any): |
| Nicknames or Titles: |
| Age and Gender Identity: |

## The Details

| Clothing and any special accessories: |
| --- |
| What do they look like? |
| Job and/or school status: |
| Hobbies or skills: |
| Three words to describe them: |
| What is their personality like? |
| Where do they live? |

## Connections

| Family: |
| --- |
| Friends and/or allies: |
| Romantic interest/relationship: |

## Deep Down: Who They Are

| What is special about them? |
| --- |
| Do they have any secrets? |
| What are they afraid of? |
| How do they react when things go wrong? |

More on this character →

## ...continued

| Character Name: |
|---|

## How They Fit Into The Story

| What motivates them? (who or what makes them take action?) |
|---|
| What are their limitations? (what is holding them back from getting what they want?) |
| What are their strengths as a person? What are they good at? |
| What are their weaknesses or flaws? What are they bad at? |
| How will they change/grow as a person during the story? |

# Draw Your Character

Or use this space for photos/celebrity casting

# CHARACTER LIST

Keep track of all your side characters: physical descriptions, connections, titles or nicknames, etc. This will be helpful for continuity throughout the whole story—so you don't say Alicia has green eyes on page 2 but blue eyes on page 100.

| NAME | NOTES |
|---|---|
| | |
| | |
| | |
| | |
| | |
| | |

| NAME | NOTES |
| --- | --- |
| | |
| | |
| | |
| | |
| | |
| | |
| | |

## FAMILY TREES

# CHARACTER NAME IDEAS

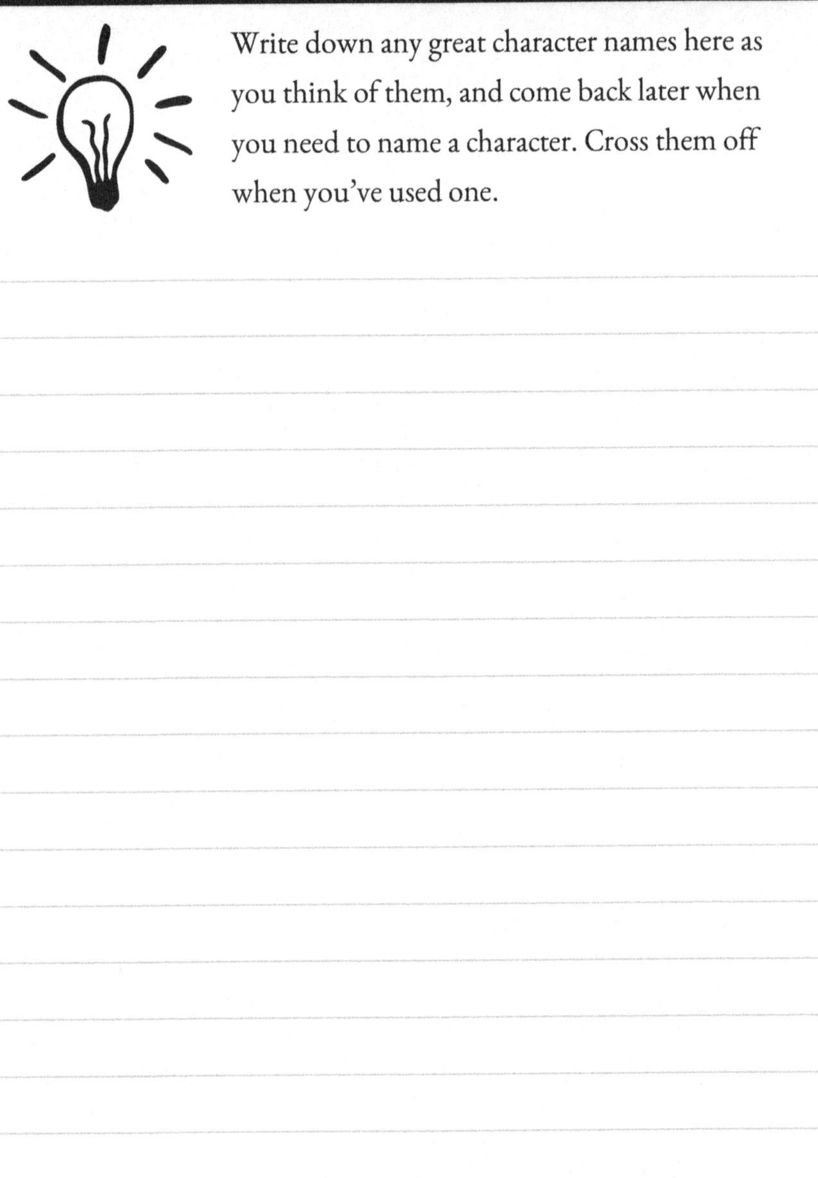

Write down any great character names here as you think of them, and come back later when you need to name a character. Cross them off when you've used one.

## MORE CHARACTER NOTES

# MORE CHARACTER NOTES

# SETTING

## SETTING PROFILE

Fill in this profile on your setting as you go, or plan it all beforehand, whatever works for you.

Your setting might not need much fleshing out if you're writing a modern story, but if you're writing fantasy, sci-fi, or anything set in another time, you'll want to keep track of how your world operates.

### The Basics

| Place Name: |
|---|
| Time Period: |
| Language(s): |
| Weather, Climate, or Geography: |

### The Specifics

| What is used for money? |
|---|
| What is the food like? Agriculture? |
| Transportation—how do people get around? |
| How are kids educated? |

| Communication—how do people talk to each other, besides in person? |
| --- |
| Clothing and fashion: |

## World Building In Depth

| Who are the leaders? Government? Politics? Royalty? |
| --- |
| Are their different class systems or factions of people? |
| Any holidays, customs or traditions: |
| What is the architecture like? |
| Is there art and entertainment? What do people do for fun? |

# SETTING PROFILE

## Magic

| Is there magic in this world? |
|---|
| Are there certain incantations or spells? How do they work? |
| Are there only special people who have magic? |
| Are there different types of magic? |
| What can magic do in this setting and story? |

For sci-fi and futuristic stories:

## Technology

| What kind of technology is common in this world? |
| --- |
| What does it do? How does it work? |
| What are the names of different devices, inventions, etc.? |
| Do different people have different technology? |
| What can technology do in this setting and story? |

# MAPS & DRAWINGS

# PLACE NAME IDEAS

Write down any great names for places here as you think of them (cities/towns, shops, streets, etc.), and come back later when you need to name something. Cross them off when you've used one.

# MORE SETTING NOTES

# MORE SETTING NOTES

# GOALS

## WORD COUNT GOALS

| | Goal: |
|---|---|
| | |
| | |
| | |
| | |
| | |
| | |
| | |
| | Half way |
| | |
| | |
| | |
| | |
| | |
| | |
| | |
| | |
| | Start o words |

Write your total word goal here.

Then write any milestone numbers down the chart. Shade in the left side as you reach each milestone.

Make up your own way to track word count here to reach daily, weekly, or monthly goals you set.

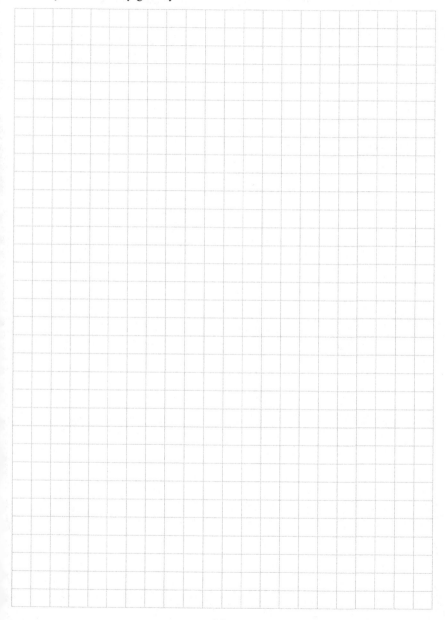

# GOALS & PROGRESS

Use these pages to set goals and track your progress. You can track daily, weekly, or monthly writing goals, and even make daily updates whenever you write.

# GOALS & PROGRESS

## GOALS & PROGRESS

# WRITING TIPS

# "How do I write a book?"

# Just write it.

There is a lot of advice out there on how to write a book, and if you've filled in this Writer's Notebook this far, you've done a lot of work already! Now you just need to put some words on paper.

**Here's some different ways you can write a book:**

- Start writing at the beginning and write until the end.
- Skip around and write different chapters.
- If you are writing from multiple character's POV, write one character's chapters, then write the other.
- Write the whole book and don't look at it for a month before you go back and read through it.

**Every writer encounters problems when writing:**

- Writer's Block
- Can't find the time
- Don't think the writing is any good

**But if you really want to write a book you need to:**

- Find a way to break your Writer's Block (see page 10).
- *Make* time to write.
- Forget about how good or bad it might be, and just write. The writing can always get better later through editing.

## WRITING & EDITING PROCESS

Here is a general outline of how the process can go, but it's different for everyone. This list is helpful for those looking to *publish.*

1. Plotting/planning (Writer's Notebook stage!)
2. Writing
3. Optional rest time (put the story away for a little while)
4. Revision: Go through your story and self-edit. You might need to rewrite entire chapters, or just fix small things. Repeat as many times as necessary.
5. Ready for readers? Give it to your first "Beta Readers"—people who read the story in its unpolished, unedited state, and can give you critique on whether the story makes sense, and is enjoyable.
6. More revision. Your beta readers probably had some feedback for you, so go back and make changes if needed.
7. Do a self-edit. Focus on finding *errors.* Spelling errors, punctuation, grammar. Repeat as needed.
8. (Optional) Research traditional publishers, agents, self-publishing, and/or professional Editors. When your book is as polished as you can make it, you'll likely go to one of those routes next!

**Don't like the look of this list?** Don't worry. You can write a book just to write one. This list is just to show the process for writers who are ready/serious about getting a book published. Go on, write your book!

# WORDSMITHING

Nobody's perfect. The next few pages are filled with spellings, corrections, formats, and punctuation tips to help you while writing, revising, or self-editing.

While you're writing your draft, you don't have to worry too much about proper spelling—just let the words flow!

| Commonly Misused Words | | |
|---|---|---|
| **Word** | **What it is** | **Example** |
| Its | Possessive of "it" | The dog chased its tail. |
| It's | It is (or It has) | It's a nice day out. |
| There | A place, or state of being | There are six iguanas. |
| Their | Shows ownership | Those are their iguanas. |
| They're | They are | They're going to pet iguanas. |
| To | Shows direction | Let's go to the cafe. |
| Too | Also | He has cupcakes too. |
| Two | The number 2 | She has two cupcakes. |
| Through | Directional | We'll go through the park. |
| Threw | An action | They threw the ball. |
| Thru | Not a word by itself | I got coffee at the drive-thru. |
| Your | Possessive of "you" | I want to read your book. |
| You're | You are | You're writing a book. |

| Commonly Confused Words | |
|---|---|
| **Accept**<br>To receive | **Except**<br>To leave out |
| **Loose**<br>Opposite of tight | **Lose**<br>Not win/misplace |
| **Affect**<br>To influence | **Effect**<br>The result |
| **Desert**<br>Hot and sandy | **Dessert**<br>Two S: think strawberry shortcake |
| **Bare**<br>Empty, uncovered | **Bear**<br>The animal, or, a burden |
| **Who's**<br>Who is | **Whose**<br>Possessive |
| **Brake**<br>What makes a car stop | **Break**<br>To rest, or to wreck |
| **Past**<br>Referring to time | **Passed**<br>A verb: past tense of "to pass" |
| **Lay**<br>To set an *object* to rest | **Lie**<br>Telling an untruth, or, to recline |
| **Then**<br>Referencing time, or 'in that case' | **Than**<br>When comparing two things |
| **Principal**<br>A person who runs a school | **Principle**<br>Belief or rule |
| **Weather**<br>Rain, sun, etc. | **Whether**<br>A conjunction |

## How to Write/Punctuate Dialogue

Check out these four different examples of dialogue, and pay close attention to their punctuation, and capitalization:

1— "I'll have a small coffee," he said.

2— I grabbed my bag and said, "OK, let's go!"

3— "Let's get in my car," Michelle said, waving, "it's this way."

4— "Wait, let me grab my bag," I said, picking it up. "OK, ready."

## Text Conversations

If you're writing in a modern time you'll likely have text messages in your story. There are actually no official rules on formatting texts. The important thing is to **always format it the <u>same way</u>**. Try not to use too many emojis or abbreviations, either. Here are two examples of how to use *italics* for texting:

— 1 —

I pulled into the bookstore and saw I had a text from Erica.

*I'm running late, be there in ten.*

— 2 —

As soon as Alice reached the path in the woods, she pulled her phone out and texted Grayson. *We need to talk.*

## Dialogue Tags

A dialogue tag tells the reader who is speaking, like these:

..." she said. ..." Alexis said.

"Said" is the most common dialogue tag, and you can and should use it widely throughout your writing. There are also plenty of other dialogue tags that you can sprinkle throughout your story; here's just a few:

| | | |
|---|---|---|
| Admitted | Asked | Demanded |
| Whispered | Replied | Promised |
| Suggested | Explained | Mumbled |
| Yelled | Told | Grumbled |
| Wondered | Stammered | Argued |
| Added | Shrieked | Drawled |
| Boomed | Pleaded | Burst out |
| Protested | Taunted | Urged |
| Retorted | Continued | Complained |
| Interrupted | Announced | Mused |

One thing you might want to avoid is adding an adverb at the end of a dialogue tag, for example: *...she said angrily.*

If you want to portray an emotion, there are better ways to do it: use a more forceful dialogue tag (*...she yelled*), or show the emotion through actions (*...she said, slamming the door*).

## WRITING THE SENSES

By adding more description using the five senses, you can:

- Make your writing stand out
- Add more words, make the story longer
- Make your characters feel more human, and your setting feel more real

This especially helps during a revision. You can focus on whether a scene uses all five senses:

### Sight — Sound — Smell — Taste — Touch

Here's some examples:

| Without the Senses | With Senses |
|---|---|
| I walked into the cabin and put down my bag, hungry and glad to be safe. | The warmth of the fire greeted me as soon as I walked into the cabin. My mouth watered as the scent of fresh bread wafted toward me, reminding me of home. |
| Dawn landed in the alley and ducked behind the dumpster. | Shock reverberated up through Dawn's feet as she landed in the alley. She ducked behind the dumpster and her nose wrinkled at the rank smell of week-old garbage. |

# "Show Don't Tell"

This is a popular phrase in the writing world. It means to SHOW the reader what is happening, not TELL them. To quote Anton Checkhov:

**"Don't tell me the moon is shining; show me the glint of light on broken glass."**

This doesn't apply to the entire manuscript (readers don't need to be shown the main character going to the bathroom, or their entire day at work, for example).

You can show through both dialogue and description. Here's some examples:

| Telling- bolded | Showing |
|---|---|
| I walked down the path behind my house. **It was winter and it was freezing.** | I walked down the snowy path behind my house, hunching my shoulders against the bitter wind and jamming my hands further into my warm pockets. |
| Keri looked at the note, **feeling anxious.** | Keri looked at the note, her heart racing as she bit her lip. |
| Alex took his phone back from Martina, **telling his friend he'd see her later, even though he didn't mean it.** | Alex yanked his phone out of Martina's hands. "I'll see you later," he lied, and walked away, his breathing fast. |

## WRITING FAQ

**How many chapters should my book be?**

As many as it needs to have. Each chapter can be a different length; some books have 12, some books have more than 50.

**How many words should be in each chapter?**

There is no rule on how many words need to be in a chapter. You might want to set your own goal range though, like between 1,000-3,000 words, that way your book's chapters are a similar length.

But don't cut off a chapter just because you're reaching your word count: end it naturally and worry about the word count later.

And some books even have chapters that are as short as one word or one sentence.

**How many words should be in the book?**

A novel is often defined as over 40,000 words. In the publishing world, each genre has its own ranges of word count (for example, Epic Fantasy can be 90,000-200,000, and YA books are usually between 50,000-75,000.

It's best to set a goal for yourself, but not worry too much about it. You can always add or cut words during revision.

# NOTES

# NOTES

## NOTES

# NOTES

# NOTES

# NOTES

# NOTES & DRAWING SPACE

# NOTES & DRAWING SPACE

## ABOUT THE AUTHOR

Liz Delton writes and lives in Connecticut, with her husband and son. She studied Theater Management at the University of the Arts in Philly, always having enjoyed the backstage life of storytelling.

She reads and writes fantasy, especially the kind with alternate worlds. Liz is the author of the dystopian Arcera Trilogy, the fantasy Realm of Camellia series, and her latest novel, *The Alchemyst's Mirror,* a steampunk mystery. World-building is her favorite part of writing, and she is always dreaming up new fantastic places.

She loves drinking tea and traveling. When she's not writing you can find her hands full with one of her many craft projects.

LizDelton.com

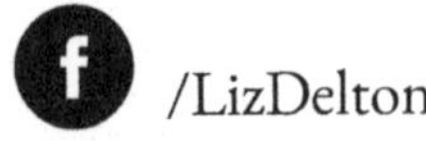

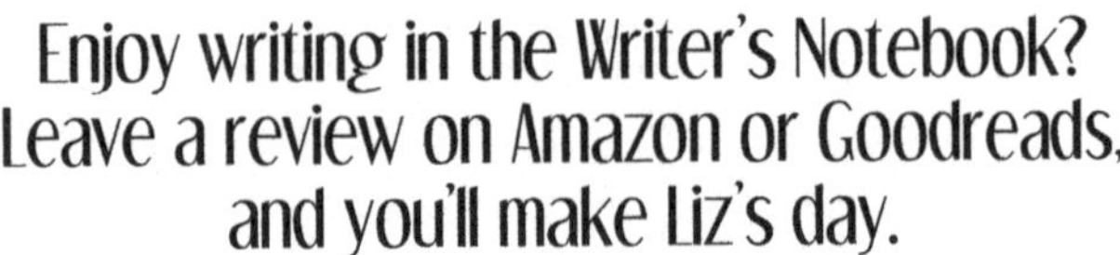

Enjoy writing in the Writer's Notebook?
Leave a review on Amazon or Goodreads,
and you'll make Liz's day.


Find more writer resources at MyWritersNotebook.com

Made in the USA
Middletown, DE
23 April 2024

53296980R00074